Our *Authentic* Selves

Reflections on What We Believe & What We Wish We Believed

BY DAVID HAMPTON

Praise for Our Authentic Selves

In his writing, David graciously demonstrates how a dualistic mindset will keep us bound to a false persona. David humbly challenges the notion that we can hide our humanity for the sake of appearances, and invites us to the beautiful and difficult work of accepting our mistakes, celebrating God's mercy and knowing the freedom that comes from a wholly reconciled heart.

~ Stephen Mason from Jars of Clay

OUR AUTHENTIC SELVES: REFLECTIONS ON WHAT
WE BELIEVE & WHAT WE WISH WE BELIEVED BY
DAVID HAMPTON
Published by Lighthouse Publishing of the Carolinas
2333 Barton Oaks Dr., Raleigh, NC, 27614

ISBN 978-1-938499-96-8
Copyright © 2013 by David Hampton
Cover design by Ken Raney: www.kenraney.com
Book design by Reality Info Systems www.realityinfo.com

Available in print from your local bookstore, online, or from
the publisher at: www.lighthousepublishingofthecarolinas.com

For more information on this book and the author visit:
www.davidbhampton.com

Library of Congress Cataloging-in-Publication Data
Hampton, David
Our Authentic Selves: Reflections on What We Believe &
What We Wish We Believed / David Hampton 1st ed.

Printed in the United States of America

About David Hampton:

Although the first bullet point on his resume would include almost two decades as a worship director at a prominent Nashville mega-church, the greatest impact of David Hampton's career and narrative isn't summed up so neatly.

David's life story is certainly highlighted by his prodigy-like talent at the piano, his awards for songwriting and musicianship, the songs and hymns he has published and recorded, and traveling with a host of well-known music artists. However, David found the theme that emerged as he became more successful was one that he would never have chosen or written into one of his melodies—and one that ultimately would offer life, hope, and healing.

The twists of his wife's suffering with a progressive and eventually debilitating disease and his own subsequent spiral into alcoholism, began derailing what at first seemed like a storybook life. In Our Authentic Selves: Reflections On What We Believe & What We Wish We Believed, David recounts with candor his days as a "professional Christian" trying to spin the plates of a very public ministry life and a serious "private" addiction to alcohol.

"If we are as sick as our secrets then I was terminally ill. I was drinking at God. I was drinking at my church. I was drinking at my wife's MS and everything in between," David explains.

"I was finding myself in situations where I had no memory

of conversations or even what happened to me the night before. My hands shook so badly I wouldn't even hand someone an ink pen," he admits. "I would have bouts of deep remorse after a night of heavy drinking and throw out all my liquor bottles in dumpsters then return later to gather up the discarded bottles to go home and drink again that night. I would wake up with pizza boxes in my bed and have no recollection of ordering, paying for, or eating a pizza.

"My wife's incapacitated state left me a virtual single parent who doubled as a nurse.

"Our daughter had two sick parents. One whom she knew couldn't help it, and one whom she thought could. She lost all respect for me and she was equally angry with both of us.

"My personal life was one long stream of broken promises. I hid in plain sight. I drank every single day for at least five years, and my life became a string of humiliating episodes that I constantly prayed would remain a secret from everyone in my ministry world. No one was more relieved than me when it all finally crashed."

David's journey into recovery brought more than just a means by which he learned to live without alcohol. He became keenly aware of his spiritual bankruptcy and all the unaddressed questions of his faith and lack of it. His story includes how he entered recovery, incorporated spiritual guides from ministers to monks, the sensory overload of fresh sobriety, and determining what parts of his old belief system would make it into the renewed version of himself that was emerging.

His story of redemption, restoration, and recovery has

offered him the opportunity to speak to a wide variety of groups including full-time ministry professionals and addiction therapy professionals, and at men's conferences, recovery conferences, national hospice professionals' conferences, and a variety of worship and arts related events, sharing his story with candor and wit.

David lives in Franklin, Tennessee. His daughter, Lauren, also lives in the Nashville area. His wife Tricia passed away on May 6, 2013 from complications due to Multiple Sclerosis.

Blog/website: davidbhampton.com
Twitter: @davidbhampton

Preface:

For most of my life, when it came to my personal faith, I could tell you what I believed about anything, anytime, at the drop of a hat. I took pride in how well I could parrot what I'd been taught about the Christian doctrine. At some point, I decided to trust the experts with matters regarding my spiritual formation and I learned to spout their words as my own. In so doing, I flipped the off switch in my heart when it came to unpacking things for myself. I didn't want to confuse myself with questions. And I certainly didn't want to explore the issues and people that fell outside the grid of what I understood to be truth.

I knew what the Christian subculture wanted, how to fit into it, and even how to make a living giving it what it wanted. I bought in, signed on, drank the Kool-Aid and even ended up working at the stand. Most confounding to me now is that I thought I was being authentic and genuine. And maybe at the time that was even true. It all worked beautifully ... until it didn't.

Most of us only *think* we own our beliefs and faith perspectives, until life blows in with hurricane force. It is then that we have to step back, rethink, reassess, and start from the bottom up.

My own story required this of me as a Professional Christian—one who made his living telling people week after week the things I eventually wondered if I even believed. My faith had become my work and Jesus had become my job. I had no categories for my wife's suffering, for my addiction, or for the havoc that played out in our home behind closed doors. What was worse was that I had no one I believed could handle hearing not only what a day in the life of me looked like, but what I secretly wondered and questioned regarding my spiritual understandings as a result of my experiences and realities.

These reflections are my perspectives from the rearview mirror after some years of grateful sobriety and the toughest seasons of my life—at least so far. These summations aren't necessarily the same convictions that I started out with and they may not be notions everyone can embrace. But they are mine. And that is more than I was ever able to say in my life before the storm.

My hope is that sharing these reflections and offering the opportunity for others to reflect will open us up to explore the difference between what we believe and what we merely wish we believed. It isn't the doctrine we learn to spout that carries us through adversity. It isn't our position on baptism that comforts us in our grief. It is embracing our authentic selves, experiencing a living God, and exercising the peace, courage, and wisdom he promises us that becomes grace for this stretch of the road.

Please take the time to use the ruled lines adjacent to these entries as an opportunity to journal your truest impressions about what these reflections expose in you. Use these forty days as a time to discern, question, and ponder what you thought you knew. My prayer is that God's Spirit would empower you with the courage to embrace authenticity and boldness. We will never be honest with others until we can first be honest with ourselves.

Contents

Our Authentic Selves:

Reflections on What We Believe and What We Wish We Believed

Day 1
Mercy Me

"Creativity is allowing yourself to make mistakes. Art is knowing which ones to keep."
~Scott Adams (Creator – Dilbert Comic strip)

I'm told that a batting average of .300 (which in baseball is considered extremely high) means that a guy only gets a base hit about thirty percent of the times he's at bat.

A medical professional recently told me that the reason medicine was called a "practice" is because it is comprised of "guesses based in scientific facts." This revealed the medical arts to be much more inexact than I might like to think.

Richard Rohr, a Catholic mystic, says that we come to God much more by doing it wrong than by doing it right.

The more maturely we look at failure, the more we realize we need it. Failure is the context by which we are reminded of our humanity, and leads us to proper understandings of our need for mercy.

I have learned a great deal from those proverbial strikeouts—that seventy percent of the time (or more) that I swing and never hit anything. I've had to recalculate many times in the course of my life when my guesses (based on what I thought were facts) didn't yield the expected result.

Allowing myself to accept my mistakes, not to mention trying to determine which mistakes to keep and call "art," is a recent hurdle for me.

Most confounding of all has been the notion that I can be drawn to God more from doing it wrong than by doing it right. To see God creating his art from what I believed to be my greatest failures is watching his mercy in action. Our brokenness is where mercy finds us but it isn't where mercy leaves us. Mercy flows much more freely from me when I live in a reality that constantly reminds me of *my* need for it.

Mercy allows me to reclaim myself and release those that I've held hostage in the prison of my own resentments.

Mercy is walking through the wounded world full of broken people, and watching what we thought were mistakes—those shattered little pieces of life—become beautiful mosaics in God's hands.

☙ Reflection: How am I willing to begin letting go of my false understanding that God can only be glorified if I'm doing it all "right"? Where are the places I see God glorified even in my own brokenness and weakness?

journal

Right now, I feel that I have an unhealthy way of dealing with failure. I beat myself up. I hate when I screw up in a performance, fall to temptation w/ food, drink too much, or forget something I need. I need grace & mercy, from both, God & others.

To start letting go of my views on failure, I can reassess how I see failure. When I give into temptation, which I will, I should remind myself of God's irresistible grace. When I screw up, I still see God's grace in my life. I am blessed beyond reason.

Day 2
Commendation, Condemnation

Picture a courtroom full of strangers. There is a twelve-person jury seated to your right and a stern-faced judge perched behind a mountain of stained oak panels. You have been called to answer for something you would rather die than say aloud, let alone confess in the presence of people you've never met.

This is the day your secret—the one you've protected above all others—is going to see the light of day. Your heart is in your throat. You can barely choke out your own name let alone speak words that address this shameful truth.

The judge somberly asks if you would tell the court the reason you stand before them. You cannot break the downward gaze that has been your posture since you entered the room. You breathe deeply and exhale the words you've never said aloud in your life.

As you confess, you begin to unpack the details, the origins, and the outcome of what you had hoped would never be spoken. You begin to loosen your gaze and lift your head to face what you believe will be the furrowed brow of a judge, the scorn of a jury, and the critical stares of every witness present.

Suddenly, the courtroom erupts in deafening applause. It grows louder, and ricochets from the floors to the plaster ceilings and back into the recesses of the courtroom. It swells like ocean waves. You hear wood scooting across the slate tiles as people back out of their chairs to stand. The judge is beaming as she joins the ovation.

You become overwhelmed with emotion, confusion, and bewilderment.

As the applause dies, the judge speaks. "We have been privileged to witness today your first steps into freedom. What you just experienced is called "grace." We are not applauding your secret or the dark details you have hidden from the world. We are applauding your courage because we know that your confession will free you. We are applauding you owning your truth and admitting enough brokenness to seek wisdom from others, and forgiveness where appropriate. We are applauding *you.*"

You learn that every person in that room has encountered a moment when *their* secret came to light, each one equally convinced that they would be shunned, shamed, and shackled for life. Each knows that downward gaze firsthand and each experienced that same ovation once they came to the end of themselves. The joy they experience now with every confession they hear reminds them of their own, and fills them with gratitude. In fact, unable to contain their enthusiasm, they erupt in acclamation.

What if we were so keenly aware of our own need for grace that hearing others confess brought about applause and joy from us? What if the confessions of others reminded us of our own and we were filled with gratitude?

ଓ Reflection: What is standing between us and experiencing the freedom of confession? What in our current belief system would need to shift in order to experience this kind of a culture of grace?

journal

I'm scared of how people would react if they knew my struggle w/ porn & homosexuality. One is shameful in the eyes of Christians & the other I'm afraid that they might tell me that nothing can be done about it. I should man up and tell one of my friends about my recent struggles. I should try to experience this grace by pouring myself out to someone.

Day 3
The Ghosts of Christmases Past

I have been going through my parents' home movies from my childhood. We look like we've been plucked from the set of Mad Men. Watching my relatives who have now passed away joke, ham it up, or even shun the camera is fun, funny, and heartwarming. I know who they all are. I know their stories. I know the occasion and setting of each frame of footage.

I had the classic, fluttery films put to DVD so we could archive them lest they be lost to the ever-rolling wave of technology. Later, it occurred to me that generation after generation would now be able to know these distant relatives, even if they won't know all of their specific stories.

While many of the people in our movies are no longer with us, they are still very much a part of us. They are woven into who we are and who we became. They existed and they mattered. They shaped us. They moved us forward. They sacrificed for us and inspired us. They failed and they succeeded. They will be a part of the reality of our stories as long as we continue to tell *theirs*. They are not just ghosts of Christmases past.

Recently, my daughter Lauren and I watched some of our own home movies from her childhood. She had come in one day and simply said, "I want to remember Mom. I only remember her as being sick and I want to remember her from before." Tricia was diagnosed with Multiple Sclerosis when Lauren was only five. As her disease became more progressive, it eclipsed most of Lauren's childhood experiences and memories.

When we watched the footage, Lauren experienced her mom in ways she hadn't remembered. She saw her mother giving her advice about how to wear makeup as she got Lauren ready for a dance recital. Lauren laughed as Tricia told funny stories while we opened Christmas gifts. There were scenes of Tricia serving cookies to Lauren's preschool class and even segments where she tried to teach Lauren to run a vacuum.

After a few hours of laughter and reminiscing together, Lauren tearfully said, "I didn't remember any of that. I only remember her as sick and removed and withdrawn. She was normal. *We* were normal. She really engaged me and wanted a relationship with me. I just didn't remember life that way. I didn't remember me that way—before I was so angry and resentful of her."

A softening happened that night. To Lauren, Tricia became more human and less ghost. Lauren saw some glimpses of her own reality that had been there all along—she'd just forgotten.

These time capsules we watch together are powerful things. It is more than visiting the ghosts of Christmases past. It may even be less about remembering others and more about remembering ourselves.

ᏣᏍ Reflection: In what ways do you remember you before you were angry? Whose story would you need to embrace and revisit in order to let go of what you thought you knew about them?

When I was *journal* younger, I was less cynical, less bitter, and more innocent. I believe that people came to me more often with their problems.

I can't think of a specific person right now who I'm bitter towards in a way that this exercize would help.

Day 4
Should

I've been thinking a lot lately about the emptiness of the word *should.*

So much of our lives are built around this word. A lot of our spirituality is explained away in this word. Should implies that there is some greater, unspoken, agreed-upon reason at work that trumps thinking, understanding, and all self-awareness by simply ascribing blind duty to a situation. *Should* is just a smokescreen that leaves us living under the illusion that we care about things that, in reality, we may not.

Should, isn't a big motivator in and of itself. "I should go to the gym." "I should drop some weight." "I should quit smoking." "I should probably go to church." "I should stop cussing in front of my kids." "I should be nicer to the lady at the dry-cleaners who doesn't speak English." "I should pray more." "I should be less self-absorbed."

Oddly, none of these comments assume any steps toward change. *Should,* never moves me from the *what,* to a *why.* It doesn't challenge the bigger reasons I'm not willing to invest myself in certain areas. *Should,* never asks me what I'm eating or drinking, who I'm angry with, whether or not I believe that God gives a rip about any of it, or if I even *want* to be more emotionally accessible. Asking *why,* however, makes me face myself. It makes me examine what is standing between me and living out what I tell myself is important. Should, simply remains a convenient little club I pull out when I need to hit myself over the head in order to feel sufficiently contrite over the things that I'm not willing to address yet.

Should, can also become a great stick by which I measure others. "He should learn to listen." "She should quit being so irritable with people." "They should be more careful with their money." "Those kids should learn some boundaries."

Should, never requires anything of me. *Should,* doesn't drive me to compassion, understanding, or to come alongside someone who is in a mess of their own consequences. *Should,* never reaches out because it doesn't have anything more to offer.

What if we replaced empty words like *should* with statements that accurately explain ourselves and challenge us to action?

What if instead we asked, "I wonder why it is that I'm eating all the time these days?" "I need to think about the resentments I may be holding against my kids so that I can quit flying off the handle at them." "I'm going to have to think about why I'm not willing to act more respectfully toward my wife and why I intentionally don't consider her opinion." "Why do I profess to believe in the power of prayer and yet I engage in so little of it?"

These are the questions that change us. It is time to press in with more honest questions. *Should,* just holds up an empty standard we only pretend to embrace.

ଓ **Reflection:** Why is it so hard for us to ask the why questions and so much easier to lead with should statements? In what ways are we afraid of the responsibility that might come from naming what is standing between what we say we believe and why we are not living in it?

journal

_____

_____

_____

_____

_____

_____

_____

_____

_____

_____

_____

_____

_____

_____

_____

_____

_____

_____

_____

Day 5
Revealing Assumptions

There is a strange climate afoot these days: assumptions are running rampant. It seems to be a season where it is okay to label, to only half listen, and to cast a wide net of opinion that goes well beyond the issues and instead demeans the character of those with whom we disagree. Worst of all, we feel the freedom to assume things about others based on the little we actually know about them personally.

Assumptions are like a false start in a hundred yard dash. It's too late once you hear the gun and realize you are ahead of the facts.

To assume is to filter everything we *think* we know about a person, situation, or event through our own arrogant grid of experience. When we assume, we are often imposing ourselves on those around us via our own unresolved issues or insecurities. Worst of all, we are rarely assuming the best of someone or some group. Most often we imagine the most sinister scenarios of those who come from outside our camps.

To have a real conversation and realize we may ultimately disagree with someone's position on an issue is one thing. To tag someone or a group of people with a certain label or disparaging rhetoric simply because they come from outside our own circle is something else entirely.

I had dinner with a friend one evening not long ago.

She lives in New York. She is from what some might call a "liberal" denomination. She is a believer who happens to vote as a Democrat. As we talked, she recounted how every time she comes to the Bible Belt, she is bombarded by assumptions based on her political perspectives or the church she attends. She said that because she is a believer, people assume she's a Republican. Or, conversely, they find out she's a Democrat and this calls all of her spiritual and doctrinal perspectives into question.

We are living in an age where believers are becoming a more and more diverse lot. Everyone in the room may not be coming from the same place politically, denominationally, or doctrinally, simply because we share the same Savior.

We need the pushing and pulling and tugging on our opinions and ideas to make us think. It is okay to disagree. It is even okay to passionately disagree. However, I don't believe that it is ever okay to assume that just because we think alike in one area we will all think alike in every area. Such assumptions shut down conversation and shut out those who might like to express another point of view.

ଔ **Reflection:** What are the areas or issues about which you think differently than you did ten years ago? On what occasions have you launched assumptions on someone's character simply because they viewed some issue or position differently?

journal

_____

_____

_____

_____

_____

_____

_____

_____

_____

_____

_____

_____

_____

_____

_____

_____

_____

_____

_____

Day 6
Go To the Wall!

After trying to articulate to some friends why I had made myself scarce during a particularly challenging season of life, I gave up my futile attempt at spinning excuses and just led with the truth. The truth was, I had hit a wall. There was no crash. Not even a thud. My emotional collision with life simply took on the form of a very pronounced but progressively dull ache exacerbated by each new calamity perpetuating it.

The culmination of several professional and personal challenges lined up like moons and stars creating a tidal wave of emotional fallout for me that, frankly, I didn't see coming. Most of these situations found me in my "do" mode, handling all the necessary details required of me but allowing myself to feel very little of the emotional fallout lying just beneath my calm, collected exterior. Being a virtual single parent, the caregiver of a progressively-ill spouse, a person living daily in recovery, and the only remaining staff member left in my department after a series of layoffs at my church, I found myself carrying a great deal of responsibility while feeling abandoned and alone.

Enter The Wall and the silent crash.

When I first assessed my relationship with The Wall and my clash with it, I realized that The Wall is the place where the spiritual realm and the physical world come together. And not always gracefully.

In Sue Monk Kidd's, *The Secret Life of Bees*, May (a pivotal character) was a broken, mentally-challenged and traumatized woman prone to deep emotional upheaval. When May would display a dark, dramatic episode, her sisters would say, "Go to the wall, May. Go to the wall!"

May slowly made her way out to the garden wall with her pad and pencil. She scribbled down the things she could not say aloud on tiny bits of paper, folded them tightly and placed them in the cracks of the mortar. For May, this was where the pain of the physical world and the hope of the spiritual coexisted. It was the tension of the wall that contained the beauty of her soul, her secrets, and her prayers.

As I began to process my own trip to The Wall, I realized that I too am spiritually scribbling down the things I want to leave there. Little bits of fear, resentment, and anger tightly folded in confessions—pieces of my heart that need healing. The concerns for those I love that weigh on me. Prayers asking God to give me my life back and at the same time fearing what it would look like if he did.

Engaging the Wall is a tangible act of prayer. Faith is seeing us place our scribbled fragments in the mortar. Salvation is when we can walk away from them, trusting that God holds those torn messages we leave in the cracks.

ఠ **Reflection:** When was your last trip to The Wall? How does this metaphor shape any new ideas about prayer for you and how we approach God from The Wall?

journal

_____

_____

_____

_____

_____

_____

_____

_____

_____

_____

_____

_____

_____

_____

_____

_____

_____

_____

_____

_____

Day 7
Great Expectations

Far too often I find that I confuse expectation with faith.

I do believe I can expect God to honor his promises. The quandary becomes exactly how and what I interpret those to be. What does God actually promise us and how do I integrate that into my faith, my personal grid for how I pray, and for whom and what I pray?

These are bigger questions than I can answer in these few words, assuming I had the answers at all.

In my own story of adversity and prayers that seemed to hover just below the ceiling tiles, I've begun to ask myself some questions. First of all, is God faithful, trustworthy, and just? Is God sovereign only when things turn out favorably from my perspective as opposed to when they turn out in ways that disappoint and even devastate me? How much of the way we approach prayer is really Evangelical superstition steeped in experience as opposed to grounded understandings about God's sovereign grace?

These are the questions I get pelted with on a very regular basis as I encounter people living with chronic and life-threatening illness, tragedy, as well as addiction and compulsive behaviors that wreak havoc in their lives and those around them. Our natural expectation would be for God to heal us, strike us sober, get us well, fix us, bring back that job we lost, or sweep in to smooth all the fallout.

God doesn't promise us that any two situations are ever going to turn out exactly alike. I also don't see that we can take certain promises in Scripture that were made to specific individuals, people groups, or cultures (regardless of how comforting and glorious they may sound) and extract them to always fit our personal paradigms. Otherwise, we would just keep the ones we like and throw out the ones where he promises to hand people over to their enemies and even allow terrible things to happen to their women and children.

I see God's promises to be in the areas of peace, wisdom, courage, and hope. Even as I ask for certain outcomes on behalf of my loved ones and myself, what I can expect is that he will grow me in peace, courage, hope, wisdom and acceptance. These things focus me on the process much more than the outcome, which I believe is really the point in the first place.

Expectation and faith are like Christmas tree lights. Even though I think I have them neatly sorted and bound up when I put them away every year, I manage to open the box to a tangled web of cords a year later. That is to say, like Christmas tree lights, I will probably be sorting faith from expectation for the rest of my life. What I am careful to remember these days is that God's promises seem to be more about carrying me through the process than about guaranteeing a particular result.

ൠ Reflection: How has your perspective on prayer been challenged in recent years? In what ways do you see God growing you in the areas of courage, peace, wisdom, and hope in the circumstances you might have otherwise prayed for him to remove?

journal

_____

_____

_____

_____

_____

_____

_____

_____

_____

_____

_____

_____

_____

_____

_____

_____

_____

_____

_____

_____

Day 8
Between Black and White

Most of us lose our authentic selves by creating personas we think our faith requires. Ultimately, we end up mistaking those personas for our authentic selves.

I'm beginning to see how many of us, not the least of which is myself, have lived with skewed ideas about who we are and what we are supposed to be about in light of living out our Christian experience. Many of us have experienced a very dualistic faith. Things are either all good or they're all bad. People are divided into two groups. Good people and bad people. Saved people and lost people. In people or out people. Not to mention when it comes to art and creativity, throwing around what is either sacred or secular. I'm either completely certain, or I'm a complete agnostic (which really isn't the exact opposite of certainty but can carry a negative connotation).

From within that kind of mindset, we begin to create our false selves. We have to. In a black and white faith the only safe thing we can do in order to fit in is to create the person we wish we were and then try to parade it around while it masquerades as us. Many of us have tried to embrace life in black and white, yet life hands us twists and turns that keep us in gray zones for which we are unprepared. Rather than addressing those challenging realities, we go into damage control. If we can't change our realities, we try to change the way we present them, or at least the way people perceive us to be living with them.

Life is anything but black and white. There are about a hundred scenarios in my life I could rattle off without taking a breath for which I have no categories or clear grids from which to live them out. I'm not always going to cope with them extremely well and I'm not going to apologize for that anymore. What I *am* doing is depending on the Holy Spirit to help sift it out.

True faith doesn't ask us to abandon our reality or the deepest things about who we are. It asks us to take the things that we are most impacted by and share them. In Micah, we read that God has already told us what he requires of us—to uphold justice, to love mercy, and to walk in humility. If being honest about our heart isn't humility then I don't know what is. Jesus said we could sum it all up by showing compassion to one another from a heart that loves God with our whole essence. Nowhere is the gospel telling us to take all the hard truth about our lives and hide it in a box in the basement.

Authentic faith doesn't require me to create a cut-out version of me that is pristine and prop it up so I'll have credibility.

ເຊ **Reflection:** Where in your life have you confused your witness with your persona? How have you tried to accommodate black and white thinking in the past?

journal

_____

_____

_____

_____

_____

_____

_____

_____

_____

_____

_____

_____

_____

_____

_____

_____

_____

_____

_____

_____

Day 9
Joy, the Kingdom, and Reality TV in Hell

I am capable of taking self-pity to some pretty creative extremes. I can conjure up some elaborate scenarios when I'm feeling ignored, abandoned, and alone. There have been seasons in my life when it was easier for me to sincerely believe that God had hung up on me than to admit the spiritual deficit from which I was trying to live, leaving me to imagine all kinds of episodes playing out in the cosmos.

I was convinced that if hell had TV, my life was playing out on their comedy network as a reality show. One at which all the dark minions of Satan were laughing hysterically—an analogy that my inner victim shared with me. I can still muster up visions of tiny ogre-like creatures getting off the sofa, brimstone smoldering under their feet, cackling aloud and wiping their eyes as they go for more popcorn. I had no idea that confronting my spiritual bankruptcy in adversity was essentially going to be addressing my expectations, my demanding notions, my concepts of prayer, and the impression of myself as an abandoned orphan of God.

I have two friends that received difficult news from their doctors recently. One friend has since learned that his news is going to be much more easily managed than he had previously feared. My second friend wasn't so fortunate and she is in for the fight of her life with what her doctors called "a pretty sucky year or so." Both friends are viewing their situations with open hands and surrender even though I can't say that either is happy about their news, nor should they be. What is remarkable in both friends is their level of anticipation as opposed to setting down a list of expectations for God to accomplish on their behalf. Both are surrounded by a loving Christian community and are experiencing the love of God in the hugs and comfort of those closest to them.

Ongoing suffering, crisis, and grief will either produce a victim or a humble heart that learns to let go of his need for answers and explanations. The victim makes demands. Expectations insist. Humility, on the other hand, can experience joy even through life's most confounding journeys because she learns to live with a loose grip.

I fear that the church often produces demanding consumers ready to become pitiful victims with rigid presumptions blaming a God who never promised them what they are insisting upon in the first place. This is why true joy is such an enigma to so many. Expectation can never know true joy because it will always be disappointed. It is based in fear and self-protection. It is perpetually discontent. Anticipation has its very roots in joy because it has open hands, looking ahead without an agenda waiting to embrace what God is going to do next. Anticipation can know peace and contentment. Expectation never will.

ᘓ **Reflection:** Spend some time pondering the differences between anticipation and expectation. What have been the consequences when the victim in you convinced you that your life was a cosmic joke? How does living in a place of humility begin to quiet those voices?

journal

_____

_____

_____

_____

_____

_____

_____

_____

_____

_____

_____

_____

_____

_____

_____

_____

_____

_____

_____

_____

Day 10
We Believe, We Believe Less

We confess.
We believe.
We believe less.
We repent.
We resist.
We confess again.

Faith seems to run in cycles at times and belief can be on a continuum. We are blinded by our pride and then humbled by the gospel. We are sincere and then insincere. Our emotions and our will continue to do battle on the furrowed ground of our hearts on a daily basis. The reality of this faith journey is that our hearts often experience something less than our heads have acknowledged. Some days we operate out of a place of trust and conviction and other days we seem to live without hope.

We confess.
We believe.
We believe less.
We repent.
We resist.
We confess again.

Rigorous honesty is vital to living an authentic faith-filled life. There are seasons when we have to admit we don't know where the road we call "God's will" is taking us. Some stretches of the road are dark and void of signs or mile markers. We cry out in the dark and we don't hear anything but the echo of our own voices coming back to us in the shadows. Yet, we believe. Maybe a little less, but we believe.

To paraphrase Thomas Merton, there are times when there doesn't seem to be a clear black and white direction, so I have to simply trust in the fact that my wanting to please God is what pleases him. I want to be in his will and yet I realize that I may not know what that is. I may even think I'm already in his will and realize later I have deluded myself. Regardless, my heart's desire is to please God, and I have to trust that my desire to please him is *indeed* what pleases him.

It takes a bold heart to look at ourselves objectively, to say we may be completely off the mark, but we are trusting God to make that okay because we have no maps for this stretch of the road. Many of life's quandaries are not in the brochure. This is where Merton's prayer resonates with me. In as much as I can ask God to impart his nature to me, I am still quite capable of kidding myself and stacking the deck in my own favor. But my heart is to please him. That, I believe, is an honest confession.

I have had to tell God many times that I don't find him trustworthy. The evidence seems to suggest that he doesn't call people back right away. I've wrung my hands in guilty fear that I missed his call and am floundering. Those are the times when something from somewhere unexpectedly speaks out of the darkness to remind me how God understands *perfectly* that I view him through the broken grid of my story. I'm reminded that I have a lifetime to learn his ways and an eternity to enjoy them.

We confess.
We believe.
We believe less.
We repent.
We resist.
We confess again.
But we believe.

Reflection: What are some choices or decisions you've had to make recently where the answer was not a clear-cut right or wrong, black or white situation? How did you experience God's pleasure in the process? How do you approach God on the days when you believe less?

journal

_____

_____

_____

_____

_____

_____

_____

_____

_____

_____

_____

_____

_____

_____

_____

_____

_____

_____

_____

Day 11
Thresholds

I have recently been doing a bit of reading about something called liminal space, or *liminality*.

Liminality isn't as spooky as it sounds. It is essentially a kind of threshold period—that sense of no longer belonging to the old and not quite yet belonging to the new. This is the season where life has moved us ahead of our plans and we are in what feels like a free-fall state. These shifts can be vocational, personal, relational, or logistical but it is always unsettling for us to be between the now and the not yet, especially when it isn't by our design or choosing.

Sometimes we aren't even aware we've entered that space until we experience the emotional fallout. As mystic Richard Rohr describes, liminality is when we have left one room but not quite entered another. This is the doorway we must walk through after life's most defining moments, the space in which we find ourselves after things like divorces, deaths, job changes, or sudden losses. And even positive shifts like sobriety and recovery. Or shifts in our belief systems or ideology that we haven't settled. Regardless, liminality is the space from which we have to address what life will look like from here forward.

Sometimes it is a season of letting go of the illusion of certainty. Most of us describe it as a crisis of faith or a time of spiritual depression when, in fact, it is just a transitional season. We know intuitively that we won't be the same but we aren't sure yet what we *will* be.

The great thing about liminal spaces is that they are where God seems to begin doing a new thing. We are no longer on autopilot and we can begin to anticipate something completely fresh. We can finally see ourselves outside of the box we've been in for years or sense a wave of God rolling us forward, away from old ways of thinking and being that we might have never left behind on our own. For all the angst and worry that accompanies being in liminal space, there is a great deal to be celebrated and anticipated.

There are multiple examples in Scripture of God leading people into such places—most often a time of teaching and preparing. This time is an excellent season to expect the fruit of deeper insights, wisdom, and compassion to follow.

Liminality doesn't last forever, so we can be certain we will eventually turn a corner of some kind … soon enough. Whether we face it with fear or anticipation is up to us.

ଔ **Reflection:** What are some thresholds you find yourself in today? What fears accompany that transition? How can you embrace a place of anticipation and joy as you watch God doing a new thing in you, as opposed to fear and regret holding on to what is falling away?

journal

_____

_____

_____

_____

_____

_____

_____

_____

_____

_____

_____

_____

_____

_____

_____

_____

_____

_____

_____

_____

Day 12
People of the Thresholds

In keeping with our focus on thresholds and embracing the thin places between who we were and who we are becoming, I would like to challenge us to embrace them as positive transitions that God will always use for our very best. Instead of fearing, dreading, or avoiding those in-between places where everything feels like it is standing still, I'm encouraged to actually seek them out. It is in those spaces that we learn to truly desire the guidance of the Holy Spirit, not just accommodate the direction should it materialize. It is also in those liminal spaces that we learn who we truly are.

I believe this is the space where the most sincere forms of worship take place. These are the places where we are basically saying to God, "Unless you show up here in this, I am done for!" It is a place of very simple prayers, honest confessions, and humble praise. Thresholds teach us that anything beautiful that has happened is a gift, any comfort is truly from his Spirit, and that whatever we experience in this interim is intentional preparation.

I'm also realizing that those of us whom I call "The People of the Thresholds" are not always the most comfortable to be around. We have so many questions, we probe beyond the stock answers, and nudge until we feel like we are a little closer to the whole truth. For those who are not in that space, it can be off-putting and even seem a bit caustic.

Ultimately, this is where we learn to trust God with the questions. This isn't where we back away from asking them or pretend we don't have them at all. This is simply the place where we are finally able to rest in the mystery. That is why worship from the thresholds is so powerful. The thresholds are the points where it is finally all about God and not about us because we've realized we have nothing to bring.

Someone asked me recently why I felt like recovery meetings seemed, at times, so much more powerful than church services. My reply was that people in recovery are desperate to be there. They know this is their last stop. People in the church, by and large, are not desperate to be there. If we were, church would look much different.

Part of any recovery model is rigorous honesty, keeping a short list of resentments, and seeking to make amends when necessary. Those are virtues learned in the threshold places. They are practices that make for authentic people and authentic worship. They don't come cheaply, but they are well-worth the time served so as to experience the freedom that comes from embracing them.

ᖴ Reflection: How can we bring the worship from our own threshold places into the corporate worship of the church? What does worship in the liminal spaces look like for you?

journal

Day 13
Altered States

How I handle my fear says a lot more about whether or not I believe God to be trustworthy than it does about what my fear is in the first place.

I believe fear drives us to create our altered states of reality. Whether it is a chemically-induced stupor or gated communities where we try to keep the world at bay, we alter reality to allow ourselves the illusion of peace and safety rather than owning or confessing our fears. If I can't confront my fear then I'll alter my perception of it. This is the reason we feel so safe in Disney World.

Our perceived securities are slowly being challenged, which is why recent cultural shifts are so frightening to many of us. Most of us bought into everything from the idea that a house is a sound investment, to the notion that a college degree guarantees a great job. Not just a great job, but a job in the field we studied.

We as a culture are being awakened from a deep sleep. I don't know if I get angrier whenever I think God is asleep or whenever he keeps waking me up from my sleep.

We have confused not living in fear with eliminating opportunities to experience it. "I will be less fearful if I home-school my kids. I will be less fearful if I live in a more secluded area with as much security as I can afford. I will be less fearful if I drive a particular vehicle because it is less likely to leave me stranded on a dark road. I will be less fearful if I work myself up to a decision-making capacity at my job so that my future isn't in the hands of idiots." And so goes our magical thinking.

While there is nothing inherently wrong with any of these pursuits, they can mask the true reasons we pursue them in the first place. How many decisions, even good decisions, in our lives are made out of a place of fear? Or, at the very least, a lack of trust?

I am the first to say I want to provide the safest, most secure lifestyle I can for my family. I will go to great lengths to adjust reality to fit what I believe to be "responsible" provision. I am trying to learn to identify, not just when those adjustments are made in fear, but what that fear really is. And what that fear says about me.

The Bible's most repeated command, "Fear not!" is not meant as a call to action (removing any opportunity to experience fear), but rather a call to trust.

ఆ **Reflection:** Examine your last few big life decisions. How much of a role did fear play? How were you able to step into a place of trust?

journal

_____

_____

_____

_____

_____

_____

_____

_____

_____

_____

_____

_____

_____

_____

_____

_____

_____

_____

_____

_____

Day 14
Potential, Maturity, and Transformation

It brings me joy when I see maturity begin to catch up with potential.

Potential, or "raw talent" as we often call it, only gets us so far. The mastering of that ability takes time, effort, focused attention, dedication, commitment, and sometimes just plain rudimentary practice.

While in the fourth grade, I went to play for the National Piano Guild auditions. I performed before a judge at our local university and received a critique afterward. I had a love/hate relationship with those auditions. I would practice for weeks and felt the greatest surge of relief when it was over. Kind of like banging one's head against a brick wall only because it feels so good when you stop. And then convincing yourself you really like head-banging as a hobby!

On this particular year, a judge called my mother in after my performance and asked me to wait in the hallway. This had never happened before and I feared I must have hit a new level of "sucks," which had previously only been lived out in my nightmares.

On the ride home, my mother asked me if I would be open to a new piano teacher, studying at the university preparatory school with a college professor, and taking music theory classes. The endeavor was pricey and my parents wanted to be sure I felt a certain level of commitment before shelling out that kind of dough on piano lessons.

I jumped at the chance. I had previously learned to fake my way through reading music, relying on my ear to carry me. I had learned poor technique and my classical pieces reflected it. While the judge gave me excellent scores, he noted that I'd picked up the habits of a lazy musician, but said that he saw extremely high potential in me.

My new instructor told me it was important to get proper training and establish good habits so that one day my hands would be able to play the music I heard in my head. Potential and maturity meeting up was life-changing for me.

Transformation is quite another matter. It comes from a deeply spiritual place and often from a place of desperation. Unlike potential, spiritual transformation seems to be more about letting go than digging in. God brings forth his vision in us when we give up our preconceived ideas about what we think things should look like.

Transformation is about progress and not performance. We turn it into a performance issue when we realize change isn't happening fast enough to suit us and we take matters into our own hands.

Transformation is authentic when noticed more by those around us than by ourselves, and it may even be the beginning of that maturity that eventually fuels potential.

 C8 **Reflection:** Where have you confused spiritual transformation with performing? How have you been able to embrace more of a "letting go" faith as opposed to a "digging in" faith?

journal

_____

_____

_____

_____

_____

_____

_____

_____

_____

_____

_____

_____

_____

_____

_____

_____

_____

_____

_____

_____

Day 15
A New Song

I've said before that I'm really a mystic disguised as a cynic who has opted for conformity to avoid conflict.

Somewhere down inside my perfectionist-driven self is a heart asking more questions than it will ever get answers to on this side of heaven. And I'm good with that—really good. In fact, I'm freer because of that than I've probably ever been in my life. It is as if God has given me a new song of the heart, as the psalms speak of. In this new song, I'm finally able to be honest with myself about what I don't know, what I believe I do know, and the blank canvas God has given me to paint on between the two.

The joy and relief that come with the words, "I don't know for sure" are freeing. They free me from defending things that make me feel like I have to memorize a handbook in order to address. I'm free from the anger that crawls up the back of my neck when people put me on the spot with their spiritual quandaries and expect me to answer them like God's personal PR guy. It frees me from trying to convince *myself* of something as I try to convince *someone else* of something. It frees me from trying to turn an "out" person into an "in" person.

I'm beginning to understand that being a believer is about loving the things that God loves, not merely satisfying a minimum requirement to get into heaven.

This new song was conceived during lots of dark nights, lonely days, silence, and literally aching with uncertainty. I wasn't sure I wanted this song at first. It evolved as I found myself in the company of other broken and honest people who celebrate life in a way I never had. This song was delivered in joy and ultimately worship as I truly sought the things God loves and, in turn, learned to love Him. Not the concept of Him or the idea of Him.

Him.

I always believed the new song would be one sung with gusto, assurance and certainty. Now I'm hearing a song that sounds distinctly different. My naïve self believed it to be a song that everyone would embrace and want to sing with me. That has not turned out to be the case. I realize such journeys are up to God, and mine doesn't make me better, more evolved, or more mature. It just tells me I'm heading down the road that God has laid out for *me*. Others may or may not find their song and that isn't up to me to enforce.

Take some seasons of silence and ask yourself if the song you've been singing is one you own and resonates with you in the most authentic parts of yourself. If it doesn't, ask God to give you a new song. Then hold on tight …

ᖑ **Reflection:** In what ways do you sense the need to ask God to give you a new song? How has the song you've been singing been one that merely parrots the songs of others or is it a song that you can own?

journal

_____

_____

_____

_____

_____

_____

_____

_____

_____

_____

_____

_____

_____

_____

_____

_____

_____

_____

_____

Day 16
Losing Our Way

"The spiritual life does not remove us from the world but leads us deeper into it."
– Henri Nouwen

I've read about a time in the early church when Christians weren't known as Christians but rather, the Followers of the Way (*the Way* as in, "the Way, the Truth, and the Life").

The term resonated with me, specifically the *Followers* part because it seemed to imply that faith was not passive or simply about getting our spiritual passport stamped. Faith wasn't just about whether or not one was going to heaven. There seems to be something tangible about following the Way, an interactive demonstration of Jesus and a proactive, intentional, and applicable faith that changed the lives of those who were touched by these followers. Following "the Way" wasn't a static, removed experience, but one that impacted those in its followers' path.

I wonder when Christianity went from being "the Way" to being a brand. When did being a follower of Jesus become reduced to joining a subculture, simply taking on a moral code that defined us, and checking off things on an offering envelope? When did we settle for an overly privatized and personalized "belief" as opposed to an interactive presentation to the world around us of who Christ is? A follower of the Way is going to exhibit peacemaking, show mercy to the poor, reach into the places where those who have no voice are ignored and, most of all, be a light in what can be a very dark world.

Following the Way implies a counting of costs. When I think of simply "becoming a Christian" it sounds a bit like I have simply changed my political party affiliation. A Democrat is an "it." A Republican is an "it." A Christian seems to have become an "it" as well. A follower of the Way, however, opens up the lid to many questions, implications, and a curiosity regarding what I'm about to embark on. It offers a compass by which I can align myself as it calls me *into* something rather than out of it. It implies a calling as opposed to simply being aligned with an experientially driven event. Being a follower of the Way puts into perspective that I am a part of something bigger than myself and that I am one among many, while the term "a Christian" can imply something singular and isolated, at least on the surface.

I'm going to give more thought to how I identify myself with the Way and examine how thinking of myself as more of a follower and less of a label challenges the things I take seriously in my life and the lives of those around me. As absurd as it sounds to say, simply being called a Christian has begun to feel a bit like I'm identifying myself with a cultural subgroup instead of a living, breathing movement.

ଔ **Reflection:** How has it felt to you to be identified as a "Christian" in recent years? How do you identify yourself as a "Christian"? What makes you a "Christian"?

journal

_____

_____
_____
_____
_____
_____
_____
_____
_____
_____
_____
_____
_____
_____
_____
_____
_____
_____
_____
_____

Day 17
Band Geeks

I had the esteemed honor of playing trombone in the marching band of William Henry Harrison High School in Evansville, Indiana. We were a band of about one hundred Marching Warriors donning red, black and white uniforms, which made us look like a brigade of toy soldiers from *The Nutcracker*.

The band was an award-winning company with a reputation for great shows, choreography, and tackling tough musical numbers while doing goose-step style running entrances and fast paced routines to intricate drum corps rhythms. Picture the Third Reich in tall, fuzzy hats being chased by a bobcat to drum music. This was a hardcore marching band and we were proud!

In honor of our noble accomplishments, the Student Council voted to award us the varsity letter sweater during my sophomore year. Imagine our delight as we wrapped ourselves in the prestige of an itchy, black wool v-neck and the cachet of the bright red H on our chests. Inside the bright red H was embroidered the word BAND in chalk white stitching. It was as if all those months of glasses sliding down our noses were finally going to pay off.

The day came when the bundles of red, black and white apparel were ceremoniously issued. We tore through the plastic like Christmas morning and immediately wiggled into our distinguished garments with a sense of illustriousness that had once only been a dream.

Upon infiltrating the ranks of the student body in our newly acquired vestments, we sensed murmuring and whispers by those from among the jock persuasion …

Panic ensued among our newly embellished tribe. There were stories of band geeks being roughed up and placed head first in trashcans. Pants being pulled to the ankles in full view of the cheerleaders became commonplace.

The food slung on our crimson H's sent the message loud and clear: we were not like the others on whom these letters had been bestowed. We were lesser than. The pervading consensus among the jocks was that we didn't work as hard, sweat as much, or deserve the honor as much as they.

Once the campaign to discredit the band sweaters was in full swing, we no longer wore them with pride, but with trepidation. We knew in our geeky pocket-protected hearts that we were worthy of distinction but it would have to remain enough that our sweaters hung quietly in the back of our closets.

I have friends who have decided to hang their proverbial letter sweaters in the back of the closet when it comes to their relationship with other Christians. They've found that every time the discussion turns to certain topics, they have their pants pulled down around their ankles or end up head-first in the trashcan of perception, leaving them to feel that maybe only believers who embrace certain views are worthy of the sweater. Rather than trying to engage in the conversation, they have found it easier to hang up the sweater.

❧ **Reflection:** When it comes to relating to Christians with differing views, have you been most guilty of either shutting down the conversation by intimidation or just hanging up the sweater?

journal

_____

_____
_____
_____
_____
_____
_____
_____
_____
_____
_____
_____
_____
_____
_____
_____
_____
_____
_____
_____
_____

Day 18
Inside Out

As I made my usual rush to the finish line in the grocery store, I saw one elderly woman with seven items in the express lane. I had milk, batteries, and an onion. I darted over to her lane knowing that her few items would have me out of there in a record three minutes. But after taking my place directly behind her, my dreams of a speedy exit soon unraveled before my eyes.

The woman suddenly began deliberating with the cashier about cake mix. It seems she preferred the one with pudding in the mix but could no longer find that version. A young sacker was quickly dispersed to see if any of her preferred pudding-in-the-mix could be retrieved. Sadly, there was no such cake mix but there was a moister version, which I learned many people prefer to the pudding-in-the-mix cakes. Who knew? I even learned that some of her church friends have switched to this and she's wanted to try it. Again, simply fascinating.

Then it occurred to her to make sure that all the eggs were intact before she left. This wasn't to be accomplished with a quick once over by merely popping up the foam lid of the carton. No, no. Each egg should be carefully inspected—individually!

Once all the items passed the equivalent of a military inspection, we were able to move on to the payment portion of our program. She pulled out her arsenal of coupons, which should have had its own Dewey Decimal System to organize. I didn't know whether she was paying for groceries or dealing out hands for a round of Texas Hold 'Em.

Once she finally paid and shuffled her way out of line, the cashier looked at me sheepishly and whispered, "I'm so sorry. She's really been slow since her stroke."

Pangs of deep regret and shame hit me.

This woman deserved the dignity of having a chance to decide the best cake mix, inspect her own eggs, determine how she spent her fixed income, and was entitled to any method she chose to organize her tattered coupons. She was out kicking life in the butt by moving outside of her circumstances. And I should be applauding her instead of tapping my numb feet.

Her life is lived from the inside out as the tenacity of who she is makes its way to the surface. She has determined that she will maintain who she is down to not settling for cake mix she doesn't want and insisting upon inspecting her own eggs.

Experiences like these confront what I see when I look at people. If I see them from the inside out I see a story. I see someone who should be celebrated. Unless we are willing to look inside, beyond the surface frustrations, we will never truly know anyone.

CB **Reflection:** Who are the difficult people in your life to love right now? How willing have you been to step into their story and see the *why* behind their *what*?

journal

_____

_____

_____

_____

_____

_____

_____

_____

_____

_____

_____

_____

_____

_____

_____

_____

_____

_____

_____

_____

Day 19
New Wine

Have you ever had an experience that changed you to your core? One that you knew would leave you completely foreign to the person you knew yourself to be before? Have you ever had to go back into some old paradigm to function as the new version of yourself only to find that the former suit of you no longer fit like it had?

The parable of the old wineskins that Jesus told comes to mind. Whether the old wineskins represent the complacency of a situation, relationships, old ways of thinking and being, or even old religious systems that cannot contain new ways of demonstrating faith, we eventually find ourselves bursting out of those old wineskins that cannot contain the life that comes from new wine.

I heard someone speak on self-centered fear this week. He said that if he had to replace the word "sin" in his vernacular he would replace it with the term self-centered fear. Patterns in his relationships, jobs, choices, habits, addictions, compulsions, and control all pointed back to his self-centered, fear-based mentality.

Eventually, he made the connection that his self-centered fear was justifying his resentments. When he realized that the resentments were fueling his entitlement, it was as if he had finally opened the lockbox of his heart and saw himself for who he truly was. As his awareness and conviction grew, he began to make huge changes in his life and relationships.

This is the kind of spiritual connecting of dots that transforms us, as opposed to merely having a faith rooted in conceptual thinking.

He realized he could no longer be as easily manipulated by his family and "friends" as he had been. He spoke of how freeing it was not to be constantly preoccupied by whether a relationship would end, a job would disappear, or whether there was always going to be enough for him. He saw himself as fully accepted by God and that he no longer needed to earn anything. Trying to please an angry God had played perfectly into his self-centered faith.

Interestingly, he says he didn't "get saved" as much as he finally began to *live* like he was. As he began to embrace that perfect acceptance, joy began to manifest itself. He said as he experienced more joy in the reality that he had nothing to prove anymore; fear began to take a backseat. The old wineskins of certain relationships that were used to encountering the old version of him couldn't always contain his new way of being. And, as old wineskins do, they ruptured.

It would seem that when we begin to ooze new wine in our lives there would be joy by everyone around us. With a heart filled with new wine comes an unpredictable and unmanageable joy. Sadly, the old wineskins of complacency can't accommodate it for very long.

ↂ Reflection: What experiences have you had with people who were so steeped in the old version of you that they couldn't accept your change? Why do you think some people are more comfortable with the fearful and predictable version of who you were?

journal

_____

_____

_____

_____

_____

_____

_____

_____

_____

_____

_____

_____

_____

_____

_____

_____

_____

_____

Day 20
Stuck!

When my wife was first diagnosed with MS, she didn't want to tell anyone outside of our immediate families at first. Her colleagues, friends, and our church family remained on the periphery of that news for some time. Eventually, there came the day when she had to reveal the nature of her disease and her unusual symptoms.

At that point, a friend said to her, "Tricia, why wouldn't you tell us? We're your friends. We want to be there for you."

Without missing a beat Tricia said, "Because I knew that once I told people, in their minds I would become David's sick wife. I knew that would become the way people described me to others: 'The lady at church with the walker.' I am not this disease. It is not my identity! I am still who I am and I want to be treated like it. I want people to still tease me. I want people to joke with me about being clumsy. I want to hear the same kind of tone in their voices I've always heard when they talk to me instead of the sympathetic tone that people take with the chronically ill. I may be trapped inside this feeble body, but I'm in here just the same and I want to be treated the same. I'm still *me*!"

I remember these conversations vividly and how she fought to maintain her identity and its place in the minds of her friends.

The Gospel of John speaks of a man lying by the pool of Bethesda who'd been paralyzed for thirty-eight years. Jesus asked him one of the most puzzling questions in the Bible, "Do you want to be well?" I believe this question was posed to his identity more than some benign precursor to the physical healing. Thirty-eight years seems a long time to lie at the pool waiting for someone to help you drag your butt into the water.

But, at the same time, I see myself in many seasons of life lamenting the fact that I can't find any help getting into the water.

What keeps us stuck this side of the pool?

Is *stuck* really a legitimate state of being, or is it when our state of mind, emotion, and will rooted in fear becomes our identity?

Maybe it is when our failures become our identity (when we literally become the sad excuses we've made) that we can't see our way out of the present and we become stuck. After all, if we tell people something about ourselves often enough they will begin to believe us.

The truth is that we are not just the sum of our mistakes or our plights. Jesus paid too high a price for us to be defined by those things. If we say we find our identity in Christ, then we must ask ourselves the question Jesus asked: "Do you want to be well?"

ᦠ Reflection: How badly do we want to be well? In what ways do you need to let the ships of failure, mistakes, and regret sail and reclaim God's vision for us from here?

journal

_____

_____

_____

_____

_____

_____

_____

_____

_____

_____

_____

_____

_____

_____

_____

_____

_____

_____

_____

_____

Day 21
Making Soup

I was recently part of an interesting discussion with staff members from various churches and denominational backgrounds on the subject of worship. Ultimately, we found ourselves discussing instrumental configurations, styles, song choices, form, and tradition, all encapsulated by the topic, "What makes great worship?"

It soon occurred to me that what I was hearing sounded akin to a couple who when asked to describe true love responded with talking about their terrific sex life.

Not much about chasing one another around the kitchen requires truly loving devotion and not much about our "great worship" makes us true worshippers. After I had challenged the conversation using my somewhat base analogy, they asked me in what context I viewed true worship.

Taking a moment I said, "We have to begin to see worship as the everyday, moment by moment things in life. Until we view things like making soup as an act of worship, we will never have a proper view of what it means to truly give God his worth with the daily parts of our lives and we will always feel as if we have to abdicate to the experts on Sunday to do it for us. We will have a very codependent relationship with experience if we lose sight of the ordinary miracles in the moment.

What the church needs to know is that when we lead

worship it is we the 'worship leaders' making our soup. We just happen to make our soup in front of a lot of people. My soup happens to include art, story, and music. Your soup may be literally making a meal for a friend who is on her second round of chemo. The Sunday Soup was never meant to be *the* soup.

If the main thing that comes up when we talk about worship is how we do it, then we are very much like the couple mistaking love for how often they swing from the chandeliers together. If our view of worship is one that understands sacrifice and living a life that matters, we are less likely to be satisfied with simply slurping down the soup someone else serves up to us once a week hoping they season it to suit our own persnickety taste buds.

I understand that when a bunch of consumers come together and decide to call themselves a church, expressions of art, music, and story in worship will be a matter of specific taste (and even propriety in the opinions of some). However, the more we can see ourselves as part of a body of past, present, and future soup makers, we can begin to embrace their various expressions and place less focus on our need to brand the soup.

Maybe it would be a good thing for our perspectives on worship and intimate relationships alike to step back from the hoo-hah and just make soup together.

Ↄ Reflection: What has challenged your views on worship in recent years? In what ways are you able to see all of life lived out under God's gaze as our true worship?

journal

_____

_____

_____

_____

_____

_____

_____

_____

_____

_____

_____

_____

_____

_____

_____

_____

_____

_____

_____

Day 22
Reality and My Doorstep

When reality finally catches up with us, it confronts those conclusions we think we've already come to on a matter. In other words, we may only think we know what we believe about something until we are actually confronted with it.

We often discover that maybe we adopted our beliefs in a vacuum. We can't know precisely how something is going to feel until it finally shows up on our doorstep. This is when we realize that maybe reality isn't quite as easily interpreted as it seemed from inside the vacuum.

When Tricia and I were newly married, we were those people who judged the young parents of children in dining establishments and movie theaters. Fit-throwing, noisy toddlers were not going to be a part of our family because we were going to make sure our children knew how to behave in public. Not too many years later I found myself carrying a screaming two-year old of my own out of an Italian bistro after she decided she no longer wanted to be there. Covered head to toe in Fettuccini Alfredo after her mini-meltdown, we found ourselves apologizing to every patron we passed as we gathered our belongings like scavengers and took the long walk of shame out the door.

Suddenly, my ideas about what I thought I would do in a situation vaporized before my eyes and the unending siren of my own child's voice in an otherwise quaint little eatery became my inescapable reality.

I used to have pat answers about divorce until some of my best friends were confronted with complicated and painful scenarios in their marriages that resulted in the end of something that neither of them had categories for nor could have anticipated.

I had all kinds of solutions about addiction and what alcoholics looked like until I woke up one day and realized "I am one."

Many of our cut-and-dried views regarding sexuality hold water until the day one of our teenaged children "comes out." Reality suddenly has a face and a name and we love them.

I find myself in a season where living wills, discontinuing curative meds, hospice teams, and medical powers of attorney are now a part of my reality. We have ventured into a new chapter in my wife's care plan as she continues to struggle. Having opinions on these matters was easier before reality took a dump on my doorstep. Even with the gift of great friends and healthcare professionals to help me think it all through, at the end of the day, reality doesn't feel like I thought it would. Reality rarely shows up dressed as it looked in the brochure. Instead, it makes what I thought would be basic cut-and-dried decisions into another peek through the dark glass known as faith.

ᛒ **Reflection:** How has reality surprised you recently? How did the way you dealt with the situation differ from what you had always believed your response would be if you found yourself in that situation?

journal

_____

_____

_____

_____

_____

_____

_____

_____

_____

_____

_____

_____

_____

_____

_____

_____

_____

_____

_____

Day 23
God, Happen To Us

There are things in life that simply happen. People run red lights and injure us. We suddenly lose a job of many years. Nature works against us and we lose homes to floods or earthquakes. So much of life seems to just *happen to us*.

On the brighter and more mysterious side are the more celebrated things of life, which seem to require much more intention from us to see to fruition.

If I choose to learn a new language, I need an instructor who will take me from the most basic principles of the alphabet to the point where I am literally thinking in that new language. Knowing Mandarin Chinese doesn't "just happen."

From a young age, I wanted to master the piano. I soon learned that my dream wouldn't come without a good amount of sacrifice. Trust me, playing Rachmaninoff does *not* just happen.

I am realizing that we as believers are asking God to happen to us more than we are seeking to invest ourselves in the things for which we are asking. We ask him to strike us sober, strike us wise, and strike us "spiritually mature" (whatever that is). "Intervene" can become code for, "don't make me have to deal with the messy part."

"God, heal this marriage!" "God, bring reconciliation between these two estranged family members!" "God, we need you to bring unity to our church!" "God, please just happen to us!"

It struck me recently that I am all about praying for things I am not willing to personally invest in. I'm tired of hearing myself pray for God to meet the financial needs of a family when I won't turn loose of a hundred dollars for them. I'm irritated with myself when I ask God to heal marriages, yet I don't want to spend an hour talking with one of the parties and sit in their pain.

I have grown very impatient with myself these days when week after week I hear people in our church tell me they are alone and all I offer is to pray that they find community. What if I also invited them to dinner?

Honest prayer is willing to grow legs.

If we are not willing to tackle reconciling with others, taking a fierce personal inventory of our resentments, or addressing the things we have done to break trust, then we can't just get into a holy huddle and expect God to happen to us.

Are we willing to get our minds out of our infirmary mentality, the place where we pray from a passive posture, and instead start participating in what God has already called us to be about?

The more we view investing ourselves as a form of prayer, the more we will see lives changed. That is renewal. It is intentional. It is already in front of us, but it doesn't just happen to us.

❧ Reflection: What have you found yourself praying for recently that you hoped to see "happen" to you? What have you consciously or unconsciously avoided taking action on in hopes that God would let you off the hook and rescue you?

journal

_____

_____

_____

_____

_____

_____

_____

_____

_____

_____

_____

_____

_____

_____

_____

_____

_____

_____

_____

Day 24
The Price of Change

A couple of years ago, I hired a personal trainer to help with the revolving door relationship I have with twenty pounds.

He was not hired to be my best friend, my ego booster, my excuse maker, or my guru. He was hired to kick my behind far beyond what I was willing to do on my own or thought myself capable of.

He had a number of catchy phrases and quips that he used to snap at me as I'd groan and come in and out of consciousness.

"Pain is just weakness leaving the body!" he barked. I countered that with, "No! I'm pretty sure that pain is the result of my dislocated shoulders after those last two military presses!"

"If you want what we have, you'll do what we do!" was another one.

Okay, I thought, maybe I'll settle for half the abs at half the price. Nothing really wrong with a well toned three-pack, is there?

"C'mon! How badly do you want it?" he'd bellow. "Not half as much as I'd like to kick your ..."

As if that would have even been an option.

I eventually reached my goal weight, but not without a major falling out. After a halfhearted workout and a couple of weeks completely blowing my food plan, he sat across from me, leaning in with his elbows on his knees. He looked me square in the face and said, "Are you committed to this or not?"

The truth was I liked the *idea* of accountability a lot more than I liked accountability itself. I wanted someone who was willing to work harder at my program than I was but not be rude enough to point that out. I wanted to redefine normal in my life without experiencing the temporary disruptions that come with long-term change.

When we find ourselves in situations where we have to redefine normal, it will always feel like suffering. It will be the emotional and spiritual equivalent of a barking trainer pushing us beyond anything we ever thought we could endure. We might even be tempted to lay blame, retaliate, and rebuff the very people we've enlisted to help us.

When the Spirit moves us toward change and prompts us away from our old normal, we must trust that God will grant us the necessary grace to walk in the new one. Whatever revival is, I don't believe it can happen in a *business as usual* paradigm. I believe it comes with challenges, with surrendering old habits and ways of thinking, and submitting to the renewing of our minds. It seems we must have defining moments as individuals where we ask ourselves, "Am I committed to this or not?"

If we are, can we risk forgiving, letting go of grudges, and releasing the emotional hostages we have taken? Can we trust that God is working as faithfully in our new normal as he did in the old one?

଄ **Reflection:** Describe your own love/hate relationship with "accountability" or, more accurately, those whom you have given permission to speak into your life? What has kept you from entering a small circle of people whom you've given permission to say the hard things to you?

journal

_____

_____

_____

_____

_____

_____

_____

_____

_____

_____

_____

_____

_____

_____

_____

_____

_____

_____

Day 25
The Gift of Assumption

There is an old adage that says, "Assume the worst and you'll never be disappointed." We've already pondered the issue of assumption from a more cultural and sub-cultural point of view, but I want to explore the tendency we have to assume the worst of the *individuals* in our lives.

If I could change one thing about myself it would be that I tend to fill the gaps in someone's story with my own negative prejudices, brokenness, and preconceived notions. I tend to assume immediately that they don't like me very much; because, on many days, *I* don't like me very much. I string together events from my experiences of the past and shoehorn them into the present. I adopt every worst-case scenario and smear them into the cracks where the grout of missing facts and truth should be.

What's worse is that often times I'm right. Many times I have assumed the worst of people and situations and been dead on. This fuels my entitlement to jump to every kind of conclusion from that point on because I don't need all the facts. After all, I have the gift of assumption. I hold it in the esteem of a talent—like juggling or being able to belch the alphabet.

There have been, however, the times when I have been dreadfully wrong. The number of times when I should have kept my assumptions to myself, because I fueled unnecessary suspicion about someone that wasn't warranted. I played on my mistrust of others to foster my assumptions and found that I and those I had influenced were completely misguided. Sadly, repentance doesn't come nearly as naturally to me as my gift of assumption. And, even after repentance rides onto the scene, often times the damage is done.

Negative assumptions thrive best in the dark, damp places where the light of trust and hope never break through the cracks of the walls. They are like the poisonous mushrooms of the soul waiting to be harvested from their dank domain at just the right moment. When the light of truth breaks through, they shrivel and lose their potency.

I have found that what disarms my tendency to jump to these conclusions is asking myself why I don't want to trust this person. Is there any history in my own life that would lead me to believe they don't have my best interest at heart? Or am I just operating in my own self-centered fear once again? When we aren't privy to all the facts, can we press pause on our assumptions for a season? There is always plenty of time to ridicule and condemn others once we have all the information.

 C8 **Reflection:** What are some ways we keep ourselves in the dark, allowing false suppositions to thrive? In what ways am I just protecting myself against disappointment by practicing the art of suspicion?

journal

_____

_____

_____

_____

_____

_____

_____

_____

_____

_____

_____

_____

_____

_____

_____

_____

_____

_____

Day 26
The Eye of the Hurricane

The eye of the hurricane is always a false sense of calm. We should never mistake a lack of conflict for peace.

When I avail myself to the eternal conversation (that which I call prayer), at some point in the exchange I'm going to ask for peace. If I'm not mindful, that can often translate into simply wanting relief. I want peace on par with an easing up of conflict, a financial windfall, or the absence of someone who is simply complicating my life. "Make it go away," is often my self-centered version of the Serenity Prayer.

When Tricia and I were first married, we didn't know how to fight very well.

That isn't true, come to think of it. We knew how to fight *extremely* well! What we didn't know how to do was fight fairly or listen in a way that didn't assume the worst of the other person.

We would have evenings that took our heated disagreements into the wee hours of the morning. Sheer exhaustion became the only thing we had in common. We faced the morning thinking we had weathered the hurricane, only to watch our discord rear its tempestuous head again in a recap over breakfast.

Wearing each other down and then collapsing from exhaustion wasn't peace. Praying it would all go away as we drifted off to sleep the night before didn't challenge the condition of our hearts. Imploring the God of the universe to magically and mysteriously cause the other person to come to their senses overnight didn't find serenity awaiting us when we opened our eyes in the morning.

Instead, what greeted us as we wiped the sleep from our eyes was the evil cousin of Serenity. The one who enjoys dressing up like her. That cousin's name is Acquiescence. Acquiescence bills herself as Serenity but at half the price. Her motto is something like, "Deny the inevitable. Eventually it will become someone else's problem."

So, how do I know whether I'm experiencing peace or simply the eye of the hurricane?

I'm learning that peace is much more about letting go than holding on. Peace requires open hands instead of tight grips. Serenity costs us owning our part in the conflict and releasing the very people we are trying to change.

If we are living in a calm aftermath that isn't accompanied by repentance, confession, and listening, then we might as well tie ourselves to the banisters and wait for the second wave of the storm to come back around.

ℭ **Reflection:** How can we discern whether or not we are experiencing true peace? In what ways can we invest the time and energy that confession, repentance, and listening requires? How can you experience peace regardless of whether others around you are able to or not?

journal

_____

_____

_____

_____

_____

_____

_____

_____

_____

_____

_____

_____

_____

_____

_____

_____

_____

_____

Day 27
Breathing Faith

"Men imagine that they communicate their virtue or vice only by overt actions, and do not see that virtue or vice emit a breath every moment."
– Ralph Waldo Emerson

Jesus came to save me for my perceived virtues as much as he did my vices. And both have proven to be considerable. I am certain that both virtue and vice can emit a breath every moment in my reality, especially if "out of the same mouth can come blessings and curses." I don't have to communicate either one by overt actions. If I breathe in and breathe out enough times in a day, both virtue and vice will be represented unmistakably. Still, somehow in the process I have this place called faith in which I find rest that assures me it is all going to be okay regardless.

A resting faith isn't a bargaining chip. It isn't about how to get the outcome I want. It isn't even really about how to like the outcome I get. Faith is acknowledging as much as is consciously possible that there is something at work I can't see, that is for my greater good. Sometimes I believe it and sometimes I don't, but I acknowledge it is ultimately true— even when both virtue and vice are competing to become an action item on my to-do list.

Faith seems to be more of a perspective to me than a state of mind I have to muster myself into. The "mustering" kind of faith is one that leaves me exhausted, depleted, and defeated and that seems counterintuitive to the peace that Christ came to bring. I can't convince myself into true faith. I often think of the times I've told someone (or been told by someone) to "have faith," to "believe," to "trust God," and to "try to let go." All of those things seem to require a mustering up that I can't quite make happen on my own, leaving me to ultimately feel like a spiritual loser because of my poor initiative.

The faith I'm learning to embrace is one that keeps reminding me that this is all about what we can't see, what we don't know yet, and are ultimately still holding on to based on spiritual apprehension as opposed to proof.

As the Emerson quote implies, we are literally capable of giving breath to both virtue and vice at any given moment. Faith tells me that God is sifting it out and uses pieces of both as he chooses for his divine purposes and ultimately his own glory.

ෆ **Reflection:** Meditate on the differences between a "resting" faith as opposed to a "mustering" faith. What are some dangers in immersing ourselves in a faith that is based in what we can conjure up by our own initiatives?

journal

_____

_____

_____

_____

_____

_____

_____

_____

_____

_____

_____

_____

_____

_____

_____

_____

_____

_____

_____

_____

Day 28
The Rock in My Shoe

By God's grace, I have been able to enjoy some consistent years of sobriety. I am finally beginning to feel the remission of regret pangs that plagued me those first few post-drinking years. I wouldn't say I absolved myself of guilt but, rather, accepted what was already done for me. The same God I drank at all those years had been weeping with me and I didn't even realize it. I have been the recipient of much grace and much understanding and for that I'm humbled and truly grateful.

What I have had to learn to live with sans anesthesia is what I call the rock in my shoe. It is a sharp, leftover reminder of where I've been, the reality of change, the reality of the things that won't, and how to get up every day and face them. When I first quit drinking, all my fear, regret, pain, and questions showed up every morning and sat at the foot of my bed staring at me like crazy relatives. It was like staring down a room full of ghosts just to get out of bed in the morning. They were known as The Committee and they used to dictate most of my decisions.

Along the way, I have begun replacing The Committee with sponsors, counselors, monks, spiritual guides, and best of all, friends who help me keep those voices at a safe distance. My best friend in the entire world remembers my sobriety birthday every year and gives me a special gift and some kind of encouraging handwritten message. That kind of friendship makes the rock in my shoe a tolerable reality and keeps The Committee from convening nearly as often.

Through my wife's illness and my own recovery I have had many people ask me how I do it. The truth is I'm not sure that *I* do. I can function with the rock in my shoe. I can smile and engage the world and even learn to walk without much of a limp. I can do my job. I can move about and I can certainly accomplish some significant things. But the reality is that I believe in a spiritual transformation that defies explanation and makes the rock more of a gift than a liability.

As much as I would love to ditch the jagged stone someday, it reminds me of my humanity and that I'm not nearly as special as I once believed. The "rock" has been something I make peace with daily, which gives me permission to be who I am. I have a beautiful and fortunate life. I am blessed with far more than I deserve. In the midst of all that, there is this sharp pebble in my shoe that not only reminds me of where I've been, but of my need for God, a guide, and a good friend to walk with me on this stretch of the road.

ଓ **Reflection:** What are the left-behind tokens in your own life that remind you of where you've been and your need for God to show up with you daily? When have you allowed them to be a gift or a liability?

journal

_____

_____

_____

_____

_____

_____

_____

_____

_____

_____

_____

_____

_____

_____

_____

_____

_____

_____

_____

Day 29
What Makes Us, Us

I had a conversation with a friend who pointed out that Jesus rarely led with the punch line. He carefully and thoughtfully drew his listeners in with the art of story. Once those around him heard the context of the story, they could grasp and own the big picture truth he had for them.

We all experience and approach life from within our own context of experience, pain, and perspective that defines our story. That's what makes us, us. But when Jesus encountered individuals, he was much more about the context of their stories than making blanket judgments or assessments of someone's life.

Sometimes theology can feel conceptual until we hear it applied through the music of someone's story; someone's unique context—that which makes them, them.

We can find encouragement, strength, and hope in one another's stories. Recovery groups place a high premium on the value of sharing stories as both encouragement to the newcomer and a reminder to the one sharing, "This is what I was like before, and this is what happened to me ..." Churches have done it forever, calling it a testimony or a witness.

I often find myself saying that God shows up in our stories. I think it would be more accurate to say that God has always been working behind the scenes, but it is when we share our stories that we begin to recognize his handiwork. When we listen to the narrative of someone else, we let go of the terminal uniqueness we have bought into as an excuse to stay where we are.

Our stories have the power to bridge the gaps between our "us and them" approach to relating with one another. There are commonalities that emerge when we share where we've been. We can call on the encouragement of one another as we reveal where we believe God is taking us. Ultimately, we see that God is at work and on the move in unique ways in every narrative.

CB **Reflection:** Are you in touch with how God has been pursuing you throughout your story?

journal

_____

_____

_____

_____

_____

_____

_____

_____

_____

_____

_____

_____

_____

_____

_____

_____

_____

_____

_____

Day 30
Spiritual Enough

I have a concern that might more accurately be categorized as a pet peeve.

I'm talking about the way we in Christian circles plug the word "spiritual" in to our language or apply it to a scenario as some kind of confidence quotient. "Spiritual" is a term that ends up being used as if it were a unit of measure. It isn't. "Spiritual" is a state of being, a realm, and a mentality. It is an awareness of the things that affect our spirit, not a mythical Disney-esqe sign which reads: *You Must Be This Spiritual to Ride This Ride.*

What is annoying to me about the way we misuse the word "spiritual" as a qualification is that it is often followed by the word "enough." This is just flat making me nuts! The scariest part of the phrase "spiritual enough" is that it assumes there would ever be a day where I am, or would be "spiritual enough." Secondly, I often hear the phrase used as a means of validating our feelings of inadequacy regarding our participation in the work of God's kingdom in the here and now.

"If I were spiritual enough …"

"I'm not feeling spiritual enough to …"

"I wonder if I'm spiritual enough to …"

We are discerning beings that God's Spirit speaks to and through, and we need to embrace the joy and the challenges that go with this. Many of us have bought into the idea that only a select form of elite "Navy Seal" Christians are qualified to tackle certain subjects or immerse themselves in kingdom life. The fact is, we don't have to know how to make Beef Wellington to work the homeless shelter's soup kitchen. We just need to be willing to dish up helpings of soup and love on people. There's nothing "spiritual enough" about it. The children's ministry coordinator at my church is constantly seeking volunteers. She isn't asking people to write a thesis on Revelation. She needs people to love kids, hand out fish crackers, and assist the teacher in charge.

If we are talking about someone possessing a level of doctrinal or theological understanding before we turn them loose on a class of new believers while teaching the book of Ephesians, that may be one thing. But I don't think articulating it as "spiritual enough" is really what we mean to say.

So, instead of leaving all the "spiritual" matters in the hands of the people we pay to lead us—the people whom we have deemed "spiritual enough" to tell us what we think, like, or how to vote—could we begin to watch for those glimmers of light that God uniquely entrusts to us? Could we own them and act on them with confidence? Could we embrace the ideas and gifts he entrusts to us uniquely as individuals, without the disclaimers? Most of all, could we accept that all things are spiritual and that we are enough?

ಚಿ **Reflection:** How have your own feelings of spiritual inadequacy been articulated in the past? How are you able to separate the word "spiritual" from a standard of measure? How is this empowering to you?

journal

_____

_____

_____

_____

_____

_____

_____

_____

_____

_____

_____

_____

_____

_____

_____

_____

_____

_____

_____

Day 31
Living Truly, Truly Living

I had a conversation with someone recently whose perceptions of hope came with some cold, hard honesty. The way he saw hope colored the way he viewed truly living and living truly.

He shared it this way:

"When I talk about hope I seem to put church people off. Because of the fact that I'm not convinced that there is really anything in my life that is going to change much, I get pegged as cynical and bitter. I want to live life fully and be one of those people who goes out and takes life by storm but I don't see that my circumstances will ever really allow me to live with that kind of abandon. I've been so discouraged by my own illness, the death of a spouse, the loss of our home, and children who are fighting over what little is left that I don't exactly see sunny skies on the horizon. It isn't that I'm bitter at God; I just simply can't emotionally afford to keep putting these scenarios before him and watching absolutely nothing change."

He stared into his coffee cup and continued, "After years of desperate tears, I have simply resigned myself to the fact that I can't afford hope. Not as far as it changing anything in *this* life anyway. You can tell me about heaven and eternity and God's love for me and I won't argue with you. But if we get down to the nitty-gritty of what I can really expect from God in the here-and-now, I'm not going to be able to buy what you're selling."

After another long, thoughtful pause, he concluded, "I'm really not angry. I'm just weary. I love the idea of hope. I just can't keep watching the wheels continue to fall off of everything I've begged for. Call me a doubter if you want to. Call me battle worn. Call me anything you need to but please, don't call me angry or bitter. I'm just tired and I can't keep living in the expectation that things will change."

I had a whole pep talk playing in my mind that I wanted to give him, and yet I resonated with that desert of indifference in which he had found himself. He would agree that this wasn't truly living but he didn't know how to live truly without acknowledging and articulating his pain and frustration the way he did.

The thin cord between truly living and living truly is strained by the tensions of our reality. Acknowledging our pain and disappointment is a part of the Christian experience. The challenge as I see it is not to let it define what we also know to be true on the other side of the dark glass of faith. Our conversation helped me to see that I don't cling to hope expecting that circumstances will change. I cling to hope because they may not!

ඟ **Reflection:** How do you define hope? How would you define living truly and truly living? How can we keep the hard realities of our lives from robbing us of the joy that comes with truly living?

journal

_____

_____

_____

_____

_____

_____

_____

_____

_____

_____

_____

_____

_____

_____

_____

_____

_____

_____

_____

Day 32
Plan A

One of the things I enjoy about working with creative people is that they understand the inexplicable tug in the soul we refer to as "calling"—the drive that pushes us to create, simply because we must create. Creative personalities don't feel much need for extensive, apologetic explanations about why one chooses to live a life with no Plan B. There is only Plan A—to create, express, and communicate truth, rattle the cages of authority, and ask the hard questions through our art.

As artists, we are often in the business of surprising ourselves. We embark on a naked canvas, an empty page, or the bare lines of a blank musical staff with nothing but these fragments of artistic shrapnel called ideas clanging around in our heads like marbles in a tin can. As the colors begin to mesh, as the lyric pours forth, and as the melody begins to define itself, no one is more surprised than we, the artists, at what is birthed.

How long has it been since we allowed ourselves to be surprised? What is keeping us from leaning into that one idea we simply can no longer excuse not doing? Are we willing to trust the Source that entrusted the spark of the dream to us with the process of seeing it to fruition? Can I trust that the One who began this good work in me will be faithful to complete it?

This thing we call the creative process is about both trusting our dreams, and *en*trusting our dreams.

I used to quote Proverbs 16:3, which says, *Commit your works to the Lord and your deeds shall be accomplished.*

I know I abused, misused, and falsely applied that verse in any number of situations in that season of my life. I tried to use it as a spiritual rationale for wanting what I wanted when I wanted it. I do believe, however, that when we experience yearnings to move forward, to create, and to invest ourselves in specific endeavors that cannot be reasoned away, the only thing to do is move forward and trust the process. We must come to a place of trusting that the same Source that is propelling us forward will see us to fruition even when the finished product surprises us.

The beautiful part about being an artist is that we know why we are here. We know that we must create and that, regardless of whatever menial job we have to do to keep the lights on, Plan A is to always follow the Source. I'm often dismayed for those who question their gifts and have never learned to trust their dream or entrust their vision. It is okay to be surprised. Plan A isn't an assurance that the work will come out looking exactly as it started out in our inspiration. It is about the process and about being willing to be surprised at where the Source takes us in it.

ଔ **Reflection:** When was the last time you were surprised by the Source? What is the dream, work, or vision for something that you have ignored simply because you didn't have a category for trusting the process or you feared that it wouldn't turn out exactly as you thought it should?

journal

_____

_____

_____

_____

_____

_____

_____

_____

_____

_____

_____

_____

_____

_____

_____

_____

_____

_____

Day 33
What Color Is Your Sky?

If one person says the sky is blue and another says it is gray, we tend to say that one must be right and the other wrong. But what might end up being true is that one person is colorblind. Their opinion is still equally valid. Gray is simply their reality.

I have a friend who is extremely colorblind. He lives life like everyone else. He just has his wife do a little creative closeting keeping his shirts, ties, socks, and pants sorted in such a way that he can tell what goes with what. He does fairly well as long as someone is guiding him along. Unless the subject comes up, one would have no idea that his reality consists of tags on hangers and socks that are placed in a certain order in his drawers. However, if he were to ignore his reality and make his own choices he would end up walking down the street in clashing color combinations, resembling the clowns of Cirque Du Soleil.

He has a few options. He can deny his impairment and strut proudly down Main Street in his fuchsia dress shirt and blazing orange tie. Or, he can admit his plight and enlist the assistance of someone close to him, lest he find himself plagued by pedestrians approaching him for snow cones and twisted animal balloons they expect him to pull out of his plaid yellow pants.

At the heart of the matter is why people see what they see.

What are the impediments of those who look at blue and only see gray? What is the broken part of the story that needs to be told for their gray to make sense to the rest of us?

I have learned to experience people in their gray as they have me in mine. I must always resist the temptation to pray, witness, or manipulate people into places that make my faith easier for me to believe. To hope that they shape up and start seeing blue simply enforces another level of expectation on them, and either forces them into performance for my benefit or denial for theirs.

There is no need to trust in an Almighty if either of those scenarios are an option.

When someone looks at blue and sees gray, it seems that my responsibility becomes about helping them sort their socks, not continuing to harp on how much better their life would be if they could see blue.

Being the church to one another is tricky business. Some of us may be the people who, for a myriad of reasons, only see gray. We are the ones who have to trust others to help us sort our socks and borrow their faith from time to time. What we can't afford to do is pretend we see things we don't. That is how we end up walking the streets in the spiritual equivalent of orange ties and plaid yellow pants.

cs **Reflection:** What have been the times in your life and story where your brokenness has left you able to only see gray in certain situations? What have been some ways you've been tempted to ignore someone's story and simply shame them into seeing blue?

journal

_____

_____

_____

_____

_____

_____

_____

_____

_____

_____

_____

_____

_____

_____

_____

_____

_____

_____

_____

Day 34
Living Conversations

My perspectives on prayer have changed in recent years. I see it in a much bigger and, frankly, more exciting context as I get beyond the idea of prayer simply being me filling the air with words at God (not just to God, but at him). No longer do I see prayer as simply laying out my laundry list of needs. That kind of praying just keeps the focus on me. It certainly didn't challenge me to learn to love the people and things that God loves even though they are out of my comfort zone.

Asking God to change me instead of my circumstances is probably the boldest act of prayer I could embark on. It is what will change the way I see others. It is what will alter my perspective of the world around me. I would much rather ask God to change others or my circumstances than to be shown what it is about me that needs to be surrendered.

Prayer that changes me is prayer that can't simply be concluded by an "amen." It is the ongoing conversation of prayer that reveals my weaknesses, exposes my truest needs to myself, and changes my view of how I really want to see my life invested. Prayer is an ongoing conversation of life with God's Spirit. For me, that is the shift from prayer merely being an exercise I felt an obligation to engage in and embracing something that I could live as naturally as breathing air. My focus went from how to "do" prayer to how to embrace it and, eventually, how to simply experience it happening.

A spiritual guide once asked me how much time I spent listening in prayer instead of doing all the talking. I have to admit I was stumped. In all my evangelical experience no one had talked to me about something as personal as contemplative prayer, silence, or the power of sensing God's impression upon my heart. What I discovered after many awkward hours of silence, boredom, and restlessness, was that I treated prayer like every other facet of my life. I dropped off laundry, picked up dinner, and did drive-through prayer. It took the awkwardness of silence and meditative practices to open my eyes to a fresh way of encountering God's Spirit.

I now see my daily life as a conversation. It isn't always a pristine one but it is an authentic one. It has only been since I began to embrace that way of being that I have sensed God challenging my generosity, my willingness to be inconvenienced, and the overall way I approach the things I see happening in the world that, "someone should do something about." It turns out that someone is "I".

This never occurred to me when I did all the talking.

ᘓ **Reflection:** How have you addressed the boredom or indifference you have felt toward prayer in the past? How can you begin to see life as a living conversation?

journal

_____

_____

_____

_____

_____

_____

_____

_____

_____

_____

_____

_____

_____

_____

_____

_____

_____

_____

_____

_____

_____

Day 35
The Price of Privilege

Picture a beautiful estate—elaborate gates, paved driveways, and enormous fountains. The grounds are beautifully landscaped and at night the windows glisten like crystal.

I'm invited along with a couple of others to housesit while the homeowners are away. In return we get a week's stay in this palatial home. The list of duties is relatively manageable; in return we are perfectly welcome to enjoy all the amenities.

We have been invited to get to know one another well. We discuss books, ideas, and even spiritual perspectives as we work together and ultimately become close friends.

Throughout the week, we get a couple of phone calls from the owners fearing there may be too much to do for the few that they've hired, so they add a couple of people to our number around midweek. I should point out here that we are all being paid an equal amount of money.

On the last day we get a call from the homeowners saying that a friend's son who is out of a job will be joining us. We take the time to show the son, as we did the few that trickled in midweek, the things that need to be done as well as enfolding them into our rich times of fellowship.

The owners arrive back at the end of one week and begin handing out envelopes and thanking each of us for our efforts. The son of their friend gets his envelope first. While everyone else is still receiving envelopes his blows out of his hands and dances across the motor court. As I lunge to help him retrieve it, I can't help noticing that the portion of the check exposed reveals the figure he was paid for his whopping one day in the house.

I realize that the number on his check for one day matched what I was promised for the entire week.

Do I get angry because he only worked one day and I trudged away for a whole week for the same amount of money? Am I going to challenge the owners who didn't have to let me work here at all, but were equally gracious to include me? Do I leave the owners in the dust and vow to never work for them again?

What if instead I focused on the great experience I had immersing myself in the lives of my fellow laborers? What if I was honestly saddened for the young man because he only got to spend one day with us instead of the great week the rest of us enjoyed—regardless of pay? After all, he missed out on the biggest part of the experience—the joy in sharing the relationships of his co-laborers.

Could the point of the story be more about gratitude for being invited into the process than what was "fair"? It is all a gift regardless of when the owners welcomed us into the process.

ೞ **Reflection:** Does this parable leave you identifying more with the grateful son who was invited into the experience at the eleventh hour, or the workers who stayed the whole week? What other categories of our Christian thinking are challenged by this story (heaven, sacrificing, fairness, God's perspective on whom he calls, etc)?

journal

Day 36
Why Follow Jesus?

I was recently told about an informal survey that asked Christians why they follow Jesus. The nomenclature in the question used terms and phraseology that Christians use to identify themselves such as "born again," "receiving Christ as a personal Savior," "making Christ Lord of one's life," praying a "sinner's prayer," etc. The survey was hoping to facilitate a kind of "Why follow Jesus?" conversation.

I am told that the most given response by the overwhelming majority of believers turned out to be, "So that I can go to heaven." I find that to be an extremely interesting commentary on us as a people of faith.

According to the people surveyed, hell is the prime motivator for calling ourselves Christ followers, as opposed to the few who said anything about Jesus being the ultimate expression of God's love. The notion that the world might indeed be a better place if I truly love my neighbor as myself and loved God with all my heart, soul, and mind, while following and exemplifying the life of Christ, apparently didn't make the top answers.

Few mentioned crying out for Jesus to rescue us from our own selfish and self-destructive paradigms. It also failed to be cited that, in turn, we would desire to live a life based in gratitude for the grace and mercy he extends to us. Modeling sacrifice and serving one another didn't top the charts either, so I'm told.

I would like to offer a simple observation: I think we are introducing Christianity as more of a series of fireproof safeguards than introducing a Jesus who meets us in our brokenness, who saves us from ourselves in the here-and-now, and calls us in to a life that is bigger than ourselves. On the surface, the survey question sounds a bit like asking someone why he or she respects their father and them coming back with the answer, "So he won't hit me!"

If our faith perspective is really all about hell, then we shouldn't act at all puzzled that we've created a culture of religious consumers who simply want to check in on our respective flavor of the month church once we get our fire insurance. Why wouldn't we? "I'll have the asbestos suite and the iron clad order of eternal security with the feet washing on the side, please."

After all, a little feet washing can go a long way.

The leper, the woman at the well, the adulterous woman about to be stoned, and blind Bartimaeus were all changed by their encounters with Jesus, but it seems it was their gratitude and astonishment in response to him that finds them living with a story they wanted to share.

Are we secure enough in our faith to take hell out of the equation long enough to ask ourselves what it is we find most compelling about Christ instead of what it is we find most troubling about hell?

ᘓ Reflection: Why do you follow Jesus? What in your own life compels you to identify yourself with Christ, apart from the supposed consequences of hell?

journal

_____

_____

_____

_____

_____

_____

_____

_____

_____

_____

_____

_____

_____

_____

_____

_____

_____

_____

_____

Day 37
The Gospel Snuggie

One of the great parts of my job is that I get to meet a wide variety of people from many different faith junctures. Many are experiencing a primary wave of God's Spirit in their lives while others are being reawakened for the first time in years.

There is, however, a wave of a different kind emerging. As Christians, we have been groomed to experience God inside the church. Yet for some of us our most significant "God encounters" of recent years have happened outside of our church paradigms as we see his Spirit moving in such areas as our recovery groups, social justice programs, and humanitarian efforts.

The realities of addiction, sexuality, equality, racism and difference-ism are being ushered to the forefront of Christian culture as we watch the conversations play out in a global forum. The culture is waiting to see how the church will respond to such issues and conversations. As Christians, we are prone to the same challenges the rest of society experiences, which brings our stories of personal brokenness and presents fresh dialogue. Our divorce rates are just as high. Our addictions are just as rampant and real. Our sexuality is just as diverse.

My concern is that I often see the church responding to these issues with a one-size-fits-all understanding of what a Christian is, looks like, agrees with, and supports socially. It is as though we are issuing little Gospel Snuggies for everyone to slip into. One size fits all. "As Seen On TV!" Everyone looks pretty much the same in it and it fits about as well on one as it does another. Most conveniently, I don't have to look at the brokenness you hide under your Snuggie of uniformity and conformity.

I'm encouraged when I watch a new generation of believers challenging what it means to be Christian and to hear people engaging in discussions in university auditoriums, regardless of whether I always agree with them or not. It encourages me to hear dialogue over monologue. There is freedom in being able to have a conversation and give others a forum in which they can say aloud what their reality is and have input about how it squares with the gospel. I believe God is calling us out from under the warmth and obscurity of our proverbial Gospel Snuggies.

I, along with many of my believing friends, am handing in the Gospel Snuggie I've been hiding under. Not for something more form-fitting or flattering either. I'm thinking of it as "clothing optional" faith. It may not be pretty but at least if enough of us do it we can begin to see that God is at work in our uniqueness and we can experience him working outside the shroud of our uniformity and conformity.

ೞ Reflection: In what situations have you been issued a Gospel Snuggie? How have you experienced authentic encounters of God at work outside of the church? In what ways would you be ready for a more "clothing optional" faith?

journal

_____

_____

_____

_____

_____

_____

_____

_____

_____

_____

_____

_____

_____

_____

_____

_____

_____

_____

_____

Day 38
Praying With My Legs

Frederick Douglass was quoted as having said, "I prayed for twenty years and received no answer until I prayed with my legs."

I am asking God to help me pray more with my legs these days. I have become increasingly convinced of late that much of what I've been asking God to do in my world is already within my grasp to some degree. The question is if I am willing to experience some inconvenience and disruption in my life to see it accomplished.

I have suffered with a false impression of how to measure God's will in my life. Up to now, the less conflict or sacrifice required, the more I was sure I was lining up with what God had for me. I even reasoned that God's will was for me to land on the side of whatever resulted in the greatest amount of happy people.

I became more aware of this unflattering reality recently when I realized the resentment regarding "unanswered prayer" that I was laying at God's doorstep. After all, could God possibly have a plan for me that would mean I couldn't maintain everything just as I've enjoyed it after all these years of accumulation, acclimation, or adaptation?

Acting on the things in my heart that I believed God wanted me to pursue would require faith, and I was praying for signs and wonders that required anything but. Like Gideon, I wanted to replace faith with a fleece. I certainly didn't factor in God expecting me to exhibit the prayers of endurance, courage, and persistence.

So, instead of embracing uncomfortable possibilities like those, I simply continued to pray with my words and dump the lack of "opportunity" coming my way on God. I eventually learned that change only happens when the pain of staying the same becomes too great. I believe a similar principle applies to our faith. When the pain of doing nothing or the fear of moving forward becomes so stifling, then I have to act on something.

If Frederick Douglass hadn't decided to pray with his legs, I don't know that his life would have looked the same and we would have missed a great figure in history who facilitated change for generations to come. I'm sure there were risks and disruptions, fears and uncertainty. Pain and misery, however, are great motivators for change. I'm sure Mr. Douglass' life knew plenty of both.

I wish I could say that my lessons testing the ropes of faith have gotten less painful, less fearful, and less paralyzing, but that wouldn't be true. What I can say is that the times I have prayed with my legs and moved outside of the stagnant sameness I found myself stuck in is when I experienced God's pleasure and found my way a little farther along the path of his leading.

◌ Reflection: What are some areas in your life about which you might just need to be praying with your legs? How is the concept of God's "perfect" will for you more paralyzing than empowering? What leaves you feeling "stuck"?

journal

Day 39
When Life Plays for Keeps

There are days when I feel like I'm playing some type of volleying sport with Life. And it seems Life does not play to lose.

Life likes to slam things past us at speeds that make our necks snap. She plays to win and she plays for keeps. The more she spikes over the net at us, the more we realize much of Life has to be lived on her terms. After all, we don't get to choose the diseases we get, the jobs we lose, or the children we have or don't have, not to mention the floods, fires, and famine that plague us. We don't get to pick our families, our gene pool, or how our ancestors were treated.

On the surface, Life could convince us that we have no recourse but to hand over the match and walk away in a quandary of confusion and convoluted thinking.

As people of faith, however, we have another piece that follows us out on to the court: the element of faith and belief. We believe that God has uniquely placed us in the story for a purpose. We believe that the purpose is to bring hope and heaven into the darkness—to leave things better than we found them. We believe that Jesus calls us to take who he is into places that don't know him yet.

I'm learning that we live in that thin, snug space where we experience pain and peace at the same time—where the pain turns out to be the peace. It is the narrow gap between swinging back and despairing that we call home.

When we view life as something to be won instead of something to be embraced, we will be in perpetual conflict. Freedom comes as I learn to discern what is and isn't mine to take on. That's far different than hitting back at Life again and again. On the occasions I can make a difference, it will be from a place of peace and conviction, not because I hit it back enough. It will be more about releasing than resisting.

Our human nature tells us when something pushes us, we should push back. When someone throws down the challenge, we pick it up. We don't admit defeat easily nor do we exhibit any surface weakness, lack of assurance, or indecision.

There is certainly an appropriate time for our God-given tenacity to be celebrated. There are certainly things worth fighting for and we need wisdom to know the difference, as the Serenity Prayer reminds us. But if I want to live out of a place of peace and serenity, I am going to have to accept Life on her terms.

When it feels like Life is playing for keeps, I am reminded that God is the keeper. I experience more comfort in the thin, snug space of *what is* when I finally quit trying to compete with it.

ᛈ **Reflection:** Where have you seen yourself kicking back at Life instead of settling in to a place of acceptance? How do we know the difference between accepting the things we can't change, and the things that should be challenged?

journal

_____

_____

_____

_____

_____

_____

_____

_____

_____

_____

_____

_____

_____

_____

_____

_____

_____

_____

_____

_____

Day 40
Our Authentic Selves …

There was a point where I had to put everything I thought I knew about God on the shelf and, with the help of some wise spiritual guides, gradually add things back. What I found was that I had parroted most of my doctrine, theology, and faith perspectives throughout my life. I repeated a "sinner's prayer" at nine years of age so I could go to heaven. I trusted the experts on pretty much everything from there and never really squared my own reality and experiences against what I was supposedly adopting as truth.

Faith was an answer-driven paradigm to me. I thought spouting off the "right" theology made me fit in and sound smart. The fact was, when push came to shove, I owned very little of it. I didn't have to. Life hadn't happened to me yet. Not real life. Not the kind that knocks the props out from under everything, leaving you standing in the rubble wondering how you got there. On the backside of those experiences, I realized I was much more of a Christian mystic than a one-size-fits-all evangelical. I had been asked to buy into a very black and white world, which was fine, until life happened.

In a black and white faith, the only safe thing we can do to fit in is to create the person we wish we were and then try to parade it around in public masquerading as us. Most of us lose our authentic selves by creating personas we think our faith requires. We therefore mistake those for the authentic. If we can't change our realities, we try to change the way we present them, or at least the way we want people to perceive us to be living them out.

God isn't asking us to abandon our reality or the deepest truths about who we are. Nowhere is the gospel telling us to take all the hard truth about our lives and hide it in a box in the basement. It asks us to take the things we are most impacted by and share them. True Christianity is stewarding our suffering. We must be about loving the things that God loves.

My life realities had left me in circumstances for which my old belief system no longer had categories. I now see God's overarching theme as being mercy—ultimate mercy that reaches beyond my imperfect understanding, choices, and even beyond the church. In his perfect mercy, there is room for our reality, brokenness, and grief. I believe God is in the business of redeeming all things to his glory by his Son Jesus, and renewing all of creation, which he loves perfectly.

My joy is in the privilege I have to be a part of it. My peace is in knowing that he can handle my reality and will hold me safely in it, and in spite of it.

Reflection: In what ways have you found yourself in a faith you don't authentically own? What questions would you ask if there would be no repercussions or negative perceptions about you?

journal

_____

_____
_____
_____
_____
_____
_____
_____
_____
_____
_____
_____
_____
_____
_____
_____
_____
_____
_____

Made in the USA
San Bernardino, CA
30 January 2014